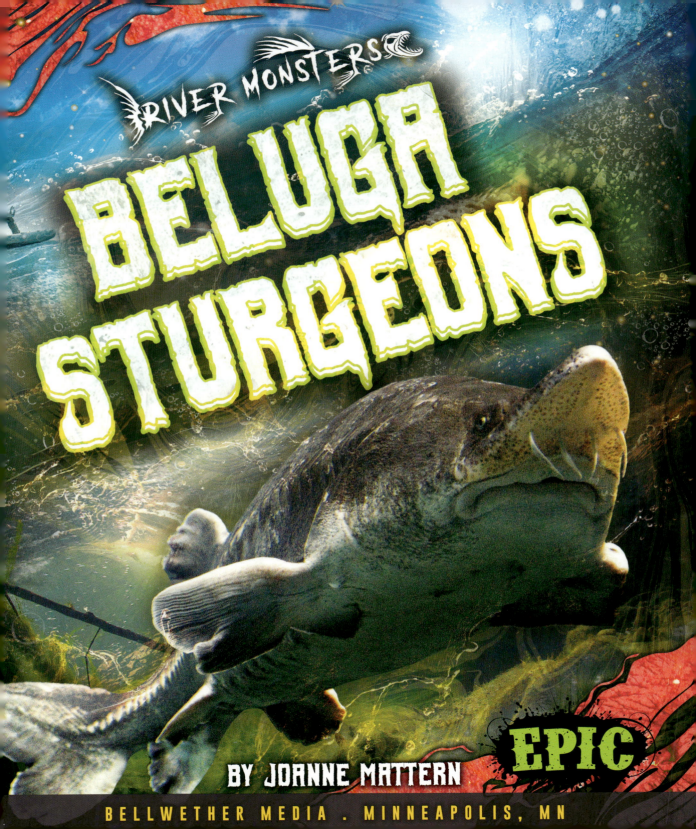

EPIC

EPIC BOOKS are no ordinary books. They burst with intense action, high-speed heroics, and shadows of the unknown. Are you ready for an Epic adventure?

This edition first published in 2024 by Bellwether Media, Inc.

No part of this publication may be reproduced in whole or in part without written permission of the publisher. For information regarding permission, write to Bellwether Media, Inc., Attention: Permissions Department, 6012 Blue Circle Drive, Minnetonka, MN 55343.

Library of Congress Cataloging-in-Publication Data

LC record for Beluga Sturgeons available at: https://lccn.loc.gov/2023039897

Text copyright © 2024 by Bellwether Media, Inc. EPIC and associated logos are trademarks and/or registered trademarks of Bellwether Media, Inc.

Editor: Elizabeth Neuenfeldt   Designer: Josh Brink

Printed in the United States of America, North Mankato, MN.

TABLE OF CONTENTS

HOME IN MANY WATERS 4
A GIANT FISH 6
UNDERWATER HUNTERS 12
STURGEONS IN DANGER! 16
GLOSSARY 22
TO LEARN MORE 23
INDEX 24

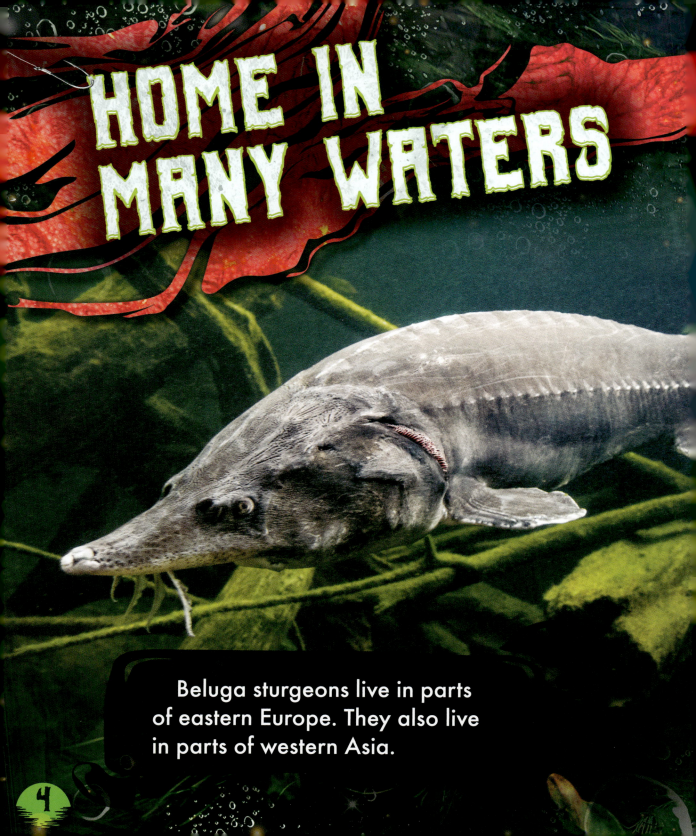

HOME IN MANY WATERS

Beluga sturgeons live in parts of eastern Europe. They also live in parts of western Asia.

They live in the Caspian Sea and the Black Sea. They swim in rivers and **estuaries**, too. They can live in **freshwater** and saltwater **habitats**!

BELUGA STURGEON RANGE

RANGE =

A GIANT FISH

Beluga sturgeons are one of the largest freshwater fish in the world!

They can be more than 20 feet (6 meters) long. Some weigh more than 3,000 pounds (1,361 kilograms). Females are larger than males.

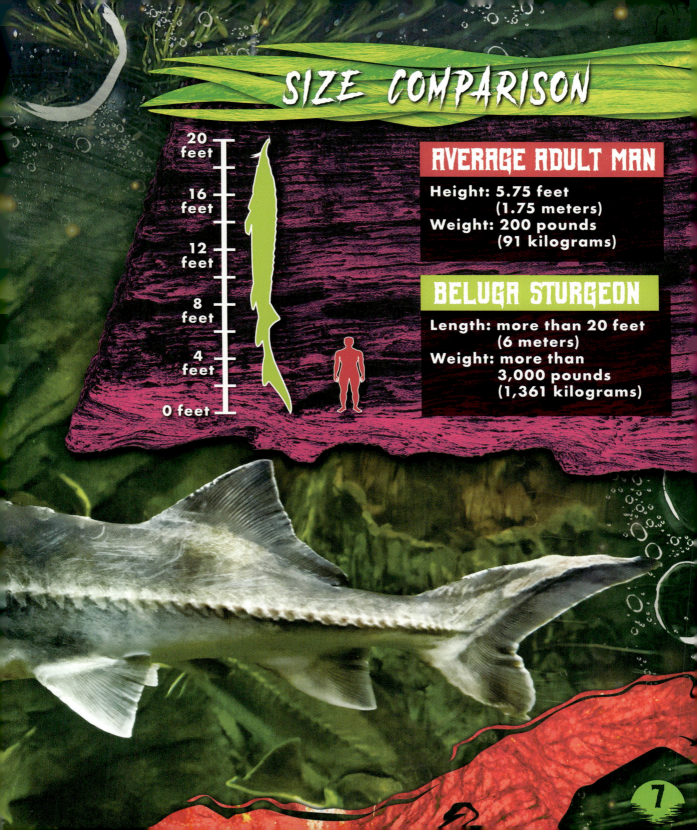

SNOUT

Beluga sturgeons have white bellies. They are black, gray, or green on top. Their **snouts** can be yellow.

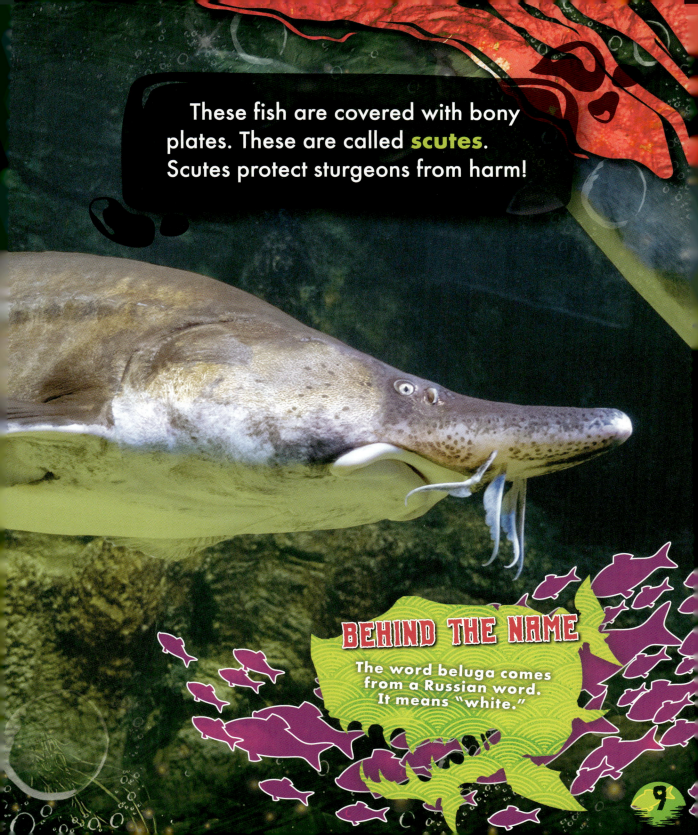

These fish are covered with bony plates. These are called **scutes**. Scutes protect sturgeons from harm!

BEHIND THE NAME

The word beluga comes from a Russian word. It means "white."

Beluga sturgeons have large fins. They have big tails, too! These help them swim quickly through the water. They have special whiskers called **barbels** around their mouths. Barbels help them find food.

TAIL

UNDERWATER HUNTERS

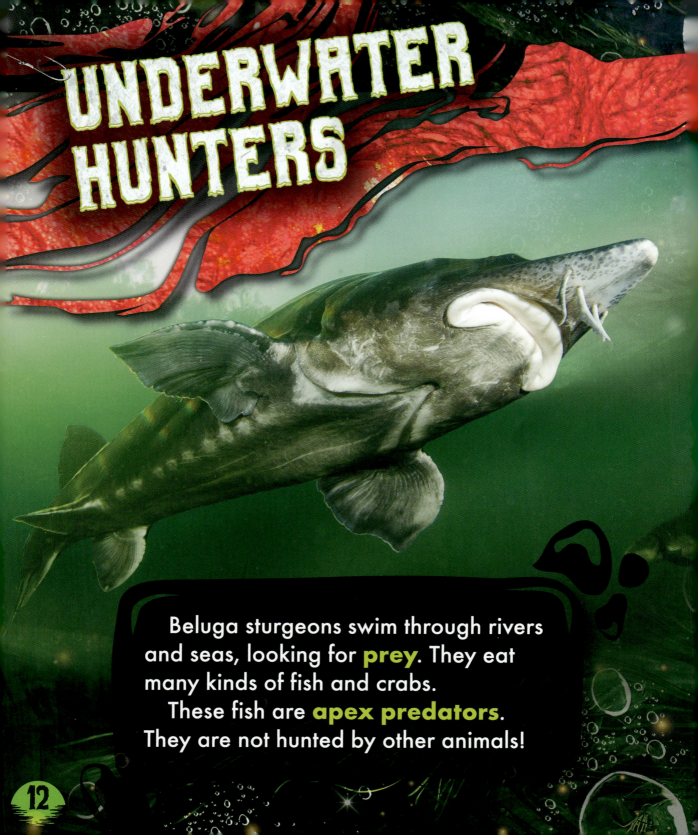

Beluga sturgeons swim through rivers and seas, looking for **prey**. They eat many kinds of fish and crabs.
These fish are **apex predators**. They are not hunted by other animals!

12

Adult sturgeons **migrate** up rivers to **spawn**. Females lay eggs on the bottom of rivers. The sticky eggs cling to rocks. Young sturgeons live on their own. They migrate to seas after they hatch.

MANY, MANY EGGS

Female beluga sturgeons can lay millions of eggs!

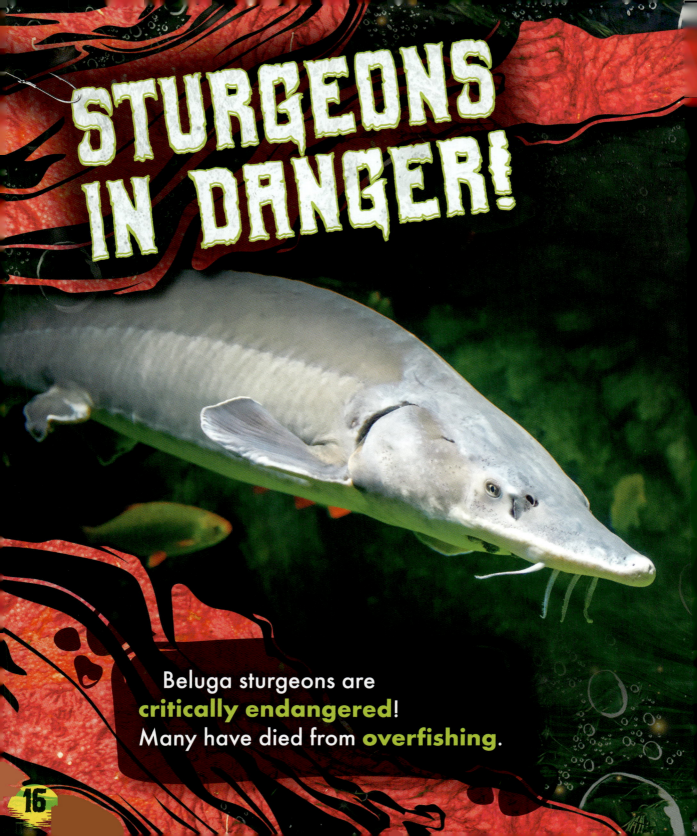

STURGEONS IN DANGER!

Beluga sturgeons are **critically endangered**! Many have died from **overfishing**.

People like to eat their meat and eggs. Their eggs are called **caviar**.

CAVIAR

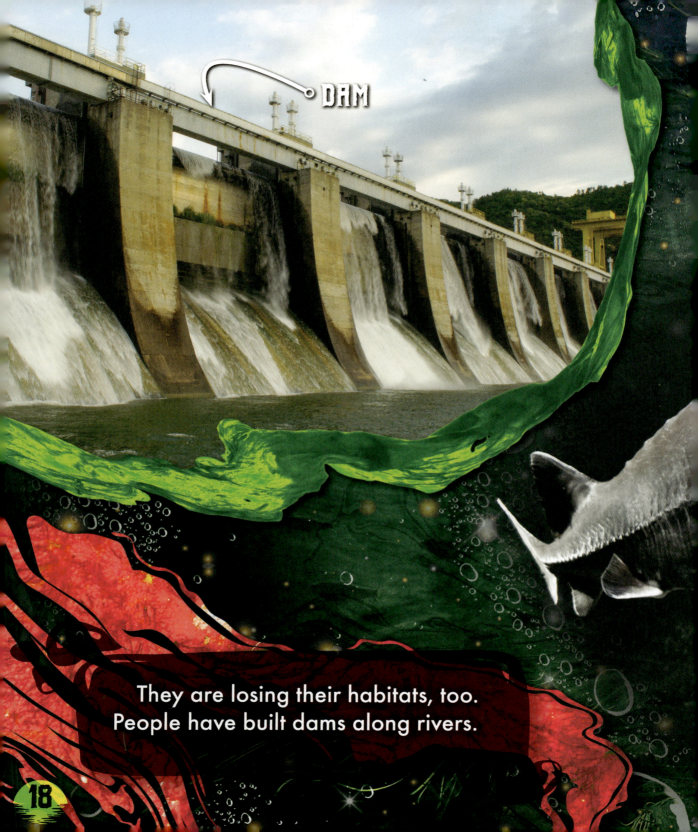

DAM

They are losing their habitats, too. People have built dams along rivers.

The dams block these sturgeons from migrating. Adults cannot lay eggs. Young cannot swim out to sea.

People are working to help beluga sturgeons. They raise these fish on farms. Then they release them in rivers. People are also trying to protect their habitats. With this help, these giant fish can survive!

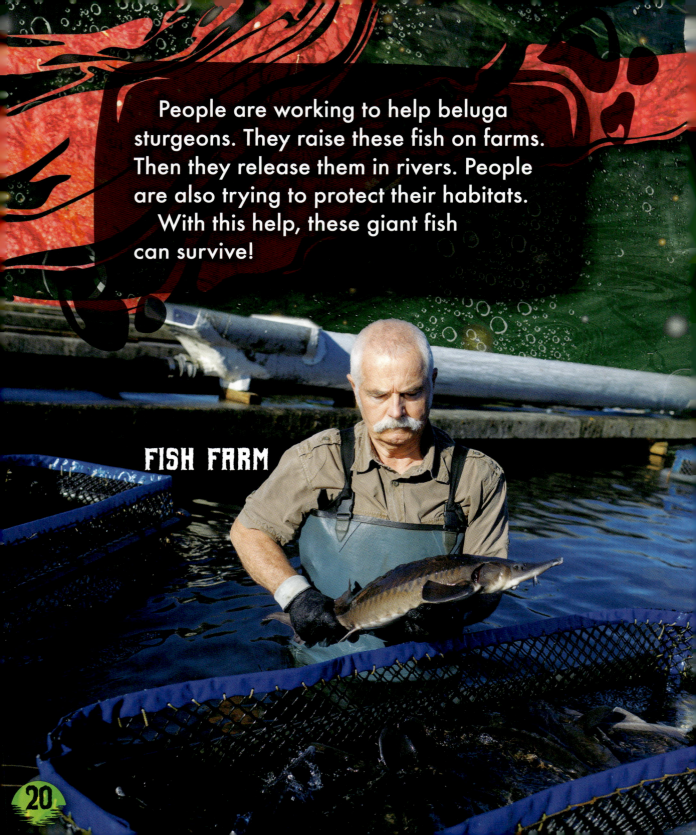

FISH FARM

GLOSSARY

apex predators—animals that are at the top of the food chain that are not preyed upon by other animals

barbels—whiskers on the lips of some fish

caviar—sturgeon eggs made into food for people to eat

critically endangered—greatly in danger of dying out

estuaries—bodies of water where freshwater and saltwater mix

freshwater—water that is not salty

habitats—places where animals live

migrate—to move from one place to another, often with the seasons

overfishing—using up the number of fish by fishing too much

prey—animals that are hunted by other animals for food

scutes—bony plates that cover sturgeons' bodies

snouts—the noses and mouths of some animals

spawn—to lay eggs

TO LEARN MORE

AT THE LIBRARY

Agnone, Julie Vosburgh. *Amazing Rivers: 100+ Waterways That Will Boggle Your Mind.* Greenbelt, Md.: What on Earth Books, 2021.

Green, Sara. *Rivers.* Minneapolis, Minn.: Bellwether Media, 2022.

Hansen, Grace. *Beluga Sturgeons.* Minneapolis, Minn.: Abdo Kids, 2019.

ON THE WEB

FACTSURFER

Factsurfer.com gives you a safe, fun way to find more information.

1. Go to www.factsurfer.com.

2. Enter "beluga sturgeons" into the search box and click 🔍.

3. Select your book cover to see a list of related content.

23

INDEX

adults, 14, 19
apex predators, 12
Asia, 4
barbels, 10, 11
Black Sea, 5
Caspian Sea, 5
caviar, 17
colors, 8
critically endangered, 16
dams, 18, 19
eggs, 14, 17, 19
estuaries, 5
Europe, 4
farms, 20
females, 6, 14
fins, 10
food, 10, 12
habitats, 5, 18, 20

identify, 11
males, 6
migrate, 14, 19
name, 9
overfishing, 16
people, 17, 18, 20
prey, 12, 13
range, 4, 5
record catch, 15
rivers, 5, 12, 14, 18, 20
scutes, 9
size, 6, 7
snouts, 8
spawn, 14
stats, 21
tails, 10
young, 14, 15, 19

The images in this book are reproduced through the courtesy of: J M Barres/ Alamy, cover (hero); Rocksweeper, pp. 2-3, 22-23, 24 (background); Zocha_K, pp. 4-5; Leonid Serebrennikov/ Alamy, pp. 6-7, 11 (barbels); Melissa Gallagher/ Alamy, p. 8; N-sky, pp. 8-9; Olga Alper, pp. 10-11; blickwinkel/Hartl/ Alamy, p. 11 (scutes, large fins, big tail); Rostislav Stefanek, pp. 12-13, 13, 14, 21; Daniel Döhne/ Wiki Commons, p. 15; Konstantin Zaykov, p. 16; Marina Tachinska, p. 17; ywanho_bg, p. 18; Mikhail Semenov, pp. 18-19; PHOVOIR/ Alamy, p. 20.